Mitchell C. Henderson

MICRO-HABITS OF FINANCIAL FREEDOM

Baby Steps to Break the Poverty Cycle

Micro-Habits of Financial Freedom: Baby Steps to Break the Poverty Cycle

Copyright © 2024

All rights reserved.
No part of this book may be reproduced in any form without permission, except brief quotations for review purposes.

ISBN: 9798304270045

Disclaimer:
This book is for educational and motivational purposes only. It does not constitute financial advice. Readers should consult a qualified financial advisor before making financial decisions.

Contents

Introduction
Small Steps, Big Changes 5

Chapter 1
Start Where You Are 8

Chapter 2
Track Every Dollar 12

Chapter 3
Break Up with One Expense 16

Chapter 4
Build a Cushion with $500 21

Chapter 5
Learn Something New About Money Every Week 26

Chapter 6
Automate Your Success 32

Chapter 7
Invest in Yourself 38

Chapter 8
Practice Gratitude and Financial Mindset Shifts 44

Chapter 9
The 10% Rule for Giving Back 50

Chapter 10
Dream Big, Plan Small 55

Chapter 11
The Power of Community 60

Chapter 12
Consistency Over Perfection 66

Conclusion
Freedom is Within Reach 71

Bonus Material 1
  Habit Tracker Templates 75

Bonus Material 2
  Reflection Questions 77

Introduction
Small Steps, Big Changes

The Power of Micro-Habits

Imagine a dripping faucet. At first glance, those tiny drops seem insignificant. But over time, they fill the sink, spill over, and can even erode rock. This is the power of micro-habits—small, consistent actions that build momentum and create life-altering change.

The journey to financial freedom often feels overwhelming, like staring up at a mountain that seems impossible to climb. But what if the secret to conquering that mountain isn't one giant leap, but thousands of small, steady steps? That's exactly what this book is about: breaking down the seemingly impossible into bite-sized, achievable habits that will change your financial future.

You don't need to have a high-paying job, perfect credit, or years of experience to begin. All you need is the willingness to take one small step today, and another tomorrow.

Why This Book?

Let's be honest: living paycheck to paycheck is exhausting. It's more than just a financial strain—it's an emotional and psychological weight that drains your energy, limits your opportunities, and keeps you stuck in a cycle of stress and survival.

And if you're like many people, you might feel trapped in that cycle with no clear way out. Maybe you've tried budgeting before, only to feel discouraged when you couldn't stick to it. Maybe the thought of saving money when you're barely making ends meet seems laughable. Or maybe you're convinced that financial freedom is for "other people," not for someone like you.

Here's the truth: You don't have to live this way. Breaking the cycle doesn't require winning the lottery or landing a six-figure job. It starts with small, intentional habits that, over time, build financial stability, confidence, and freedom.

This book is your roadmap. It's not about quick fixes or impossible promises. Instead, it's about real, actionable steps that anyone can take—regardless of income or starting point.

What to Expect

Each chapter in this book introduces a small, achievable habit that builds on the last. These aren't just "good ideas" or wishful thinking—they're proven strategies designed to create real change, even if you're starting from zero.

Here's what you'll learn:

- How to start saving with as little as $1 a day.
- Simple ways to track your spending and cut out unnecessary expenses.
- How to build an emergency fund, get out of debt, and start investing—even on a tight budget.
- The emotional and psychological shifts needed to break free from a scarcity mindset.

But more than that, you'll learn how to take control of your money—and your life—one small step at a time.

This isn't just about money. It's about breaking free from the limitations that have held you back and creating a life of purpose, possibility, and security. By the end of this book, you won't just have a list of habits—you'll have a new way of thinking about money, success, and your own potential.

Are you ready? Let's take that first step together.

Chapter 1
Start Where You Are

The Courage to Begin

Every journey starts with a single step. That may sound cliché, but when it comes to breaking the poverty cycle, it's profoundly true. You don't have to have it all figured out. You don't need a perfect plan or even extra money sitting around. You just need to start. Right now.

Here's the reality: Financial freedom isn't about where you've been. It's about where you're going—and the small, intentional choices you make along the way. The first step? Assessing where you are today.

Assessing Your Financial Situation Without Shame

Taking a hard look at your finances can feel intimidating, even painful. Maybe you're carrying debt that feels suffocating. Maybe your paycheck seems to vanish the moment it hits your account. Or maybe you've been avoiding your bank statements altogether, hoping the problem will somehow fix itself.

Let me tell you something important: There is no shame in your starting point. Whether you're drowning in debt, living paycheck to paycheck, or feeling like you'll never get ahead, you're not alone. And you're not stuck.

The key is to face your finances with honesty and without guilt. Guilt keeps you stuck in the past. Honesty lets you build a better future.

Take a deep breath and write down three things:

1. Your total income.
2. Your total expenses.
3. Any debts or savings you have.

This is your financial snapshot—a clear picture of where you are today. It's not about judgment; it's about awareness. Because once you know where you are, you can start moving forward.

The "$1 a Day" Habit: Starting Small, Dreaming Big

Now that you've assessed your situation, it's time to take action. And that action starts small—really small.

Can you save $1 today? That's it. Just one dollar.

Here's why this habit matters: Saving $1 a day isn't about the amount; it's about building momentum. It's about proving to yourself that you *can* save, even if your budget feels tight. Over time, that $1 adds up—not just in dollars, but in confidence and consistency.

Think about it:

- $1 a day becomes $30 a month.
- In a year, you'll have $365 saved.
- If you can increase that amount even slightly, the growth multiplies.

But more importantly, this habit builds discipline and rewires your mindset. You're no longer someone who "can't save." You're someone who does.

How to Make It Happen

Here are a few practical ways to start your $1 a day habit:

- **Open a Savings Account**: If you don't already have one, open a separate account specifically for your $1 a day savings. Automate the transfer if possible.
- **Create a Savings Jar**: If you prefer something tangible, grab an empty jar, label it "My Freedom Fund," and drop in your first dollar.
- **Use a Budgeting App**: Many apps let you set small savings goals and track your progress. Find one that works for you.

The method doesn't matter as much as the action. What matters is that you're taking control, one dollar at a time.

Quick Action Step

Right now—before you turn to the next chapter—commit to saving your first $1. Whether it's a dollar bill in a jar, an electronic transfer to a savings account, or a note on your phone reminding you to start tomorrow, make the commitment.

This is your first step toward financial freedom. It's small, but it's powerful. Because from this moment on, you're no longer standing still. You're moving forward.

Are you ready to take the next step? Let's keep building this momentum. The journey has just begun.

Chapter 2

Track Every Dollar

The First Step to Mastering Your Money

Have you ever looked at your bank account and wondered, *Where did all my money go?* If so, you're not alone. Most people don't realize just how much they spend—or how they spend it—until they start paying attention.

The truth is, you can't change what you don't track. If you want to take control of your finances, the first step is understanding exactly where your money is going.

Why Tracking Matters

Tracking every dollar isn't just a habit—it's a revelation. It gives you a clear picture of your spending patterns, helps you identify wasteful habits, and reveals opportunities to save.

When you track your money, you gain control over it. Instead of wondering where your money went, you can decide where it *will* go.

Think of tracking as shining a light into a dark room. Once you can see clearly, you'll know what to keep, what to change, and what to let go of.

The One-Week Challenge: Track Every Expense

You don't have to commit to tracking forever—just start with one week. For the next seven days, write down *every single expense*. Yes, every single one. That $2 coffee? Write it down. The $20 you spent on takeout? Write it down. The unexpected $50 gas bill? Write it down.

This is your micro-habit: Keep a record of where your money goes, no matter how small the amount.

Here's what you'll discover:

1. **Patterns:** Are there areas where you're spending more than you realized?
2. **Priorities:** Are you spending money on what truly matters to you?
3. **Potential Savings:** Are there expenses you could cut without feeling deprived?

By the end of the week, you'll have a clear snapshot of your spending—and the insights you need to make changes.

How to Track Every Dollar

You don't need fancy tools to get started. Use whatever method feels easiest and most natural for you:

- **A Simple Notebook:** Keep a small notebook in your bag or pocket and jot down every expense as it happens.
- **Budgeting Apps:** Apps like Mint, YNAB (You Need a Budget), or PocketGuard can link to your bank account and categorize your spending automatically.
- **A Spreadsheet:** If you prefer a digital approach, create a simple spreadsheet to log your expenses.
- **Receipts:** Save your receipts and review them at the end of each day to log your purchases.

The key isn't the tool—it's the consistency. Commit to tracking every expense for one week.

The Power of Awareness

At first, tracking every dollar might feel tedious, even uncomfortable. That's normal. But stick with it. Because the moment you see where your money is going, you'll feel empowered to take control.

You might realize you're spending more on dining out than you thought. Or maybe you'll see that your monthly subscription fees are adding up fast. Whatever you discover, it's not about judgment—it's about awareness.

When you know better, you can do better. Tracking every dollar gives you the knowledge you need to make smarter choices and create a spending plan that works for your life.

Quick Action Step

Don't wait—start your one-week tracking challenge today. Grab a notebook, download an app, or open a spreadsheet. Set a reminder on your phone to log your expenses daily.

At the end of the week, take 10 minutes to review your spending. Highlight one or two areas where you could cut back or reallocate funds to something more meaningful.

This simple habit can transform the way you think about money. Because when you track every dollar, you take the first step toward making every dollar work for you.

Let's keep building on this momentum—your financial transformation is just getting started.

Chapter 3
Break Up with One Expense

Small Cuts, Big Gains

Financial freedom doesn't start with grand gestures—it starts with one small decision. Sometimes, all it takes to shift your money mindset is breaking up with a single expense that's holding you back.

We all have those little costs that sneak into our budgets: the daily coffee run, the streaming subscription you rarely use, or the gym membership that's been gathering dust. These expenses seem harmless on their own, but over time, they add up to a significant drain on your finances.

It's time to let one of them go—not because you have to, but because you *choose to.*

The Hidden Power of Cutting One Expense

When you decide to cut an unnecessary expense, you're doing more than saving money—you're reclaiming control. This is a deliberate act of prioritizing your long-term goals over instant gratification.

Imagine cutting a $5-a-day coffee habit. That's $35 a week, $150 a month, and nearly $2,000 a year. Redirecting even a small amount like this can help you pay down debt faster, build your emergency fund, or start investing in your future.

The point isn't deprivation; it's empowerment. You're taking an active step toward financial freedom.

How to Identify the Right Expense

The key is to choose one expense that:

1. **Doesn't add real value to your life:** Is it something you could live without and not miss?
2. **Has a clear alternative:** For example, brewing coffee at home instead of buying it on the go.
3. **Fits your financial goals:** Redirecting this money toward savings, debt, or another priority should feel rewarding.

Here's a simple exercise: Look at your bank statements or expense tracker from the past month. Highlight one recurring expense or category that isn't essential or deeply meaningful.

Ask yourself:

- Does this bring me joy or just convenience?
- Could I replace this with a cheaper alternative?
- How much could I save over time by letting this go?

The Micro-Habit: Redirecting Your Savings

Cutting the expense is only half the battle. The real magic happens when you redirect that money toward something meaningful.

Let's say you cut a $20-a-month subscription you barely use. Instead of letting that $20 disappear into other expenses, set up an automatic transfer into your savings account or use it to pay off a small chunk of debt.

This small habit has a compounding effect. Over time, the money you save grows—and so does your sense of accomplishment.

Reflection: The Ripple Effect of Small Choices

Cutting one expense might not seem like a big deal, but it's part of a bigger shift. It's proof that you have the power to make intentional choices with your money.

Consider this: If you can let go of one unnecessary expense, what else could you change? Maybe you'll realize you don't need that extra streaming service, or that dining out twice a week could become once a week.

Each small change creates breathing room in your budget, reduces stress, and brings you closer to your financial goals.

Breaking Up Doesn't Have to Be Hard

If the thought of cutting an expense feels difficult, remind yourself: This isn't about saying "no" forever—it's about saying "yes" to something better.

Picture the life you're working toward. Imagine the weight of financial stress lifting as you build your savings or pay off debt. That vision is worth the small sacrifice of letting go of one expense today.

Quick Action Step

1. Identify one unnecessary expense you can cut this week.
2. Decide where to redirect the money—savings, debt repayment, or another financial goal.
3. Set a reminder to revisit your budget in a month and celebrate your progress.

Remember, this is just the beginning. Every small step you take builds momentum, and every dollar you save moves you closer to freedom.

The journey out of the poverty cycle starts here—with one simple, intentional choice. Let's keep going. You're building something incredible!

Chapter 4
Build a Cushion with $500

Your First Step Toward Financial Stability

Imagine this: Your car breaks down, and you need $300 for repairs. Without a financial cushion, this could mean maxing out a credit card, borrowing money, or worse—going without transportation. But what if you had $500 set aside, ready to handle the unexpected?

That's the power of a small emergency fund. It's not about solving all your financial problems at once. It's about creating a safety net that gives you breathing room and confidence to face life's challenges without panic.

Let's make that $500 happen—one small step at a time.

Why $500 is a Game-Changer

For many people, $500 can feel like a small fortune, especially if they've been living paycheck to paycheck. But here's the good news: You don't need thousands of dollars to start feeling the benefits of financial stability.

That initial $500 does three powerful things:

1. **Breaks the cycle of relying on credit cards or loans:** It covers minor emergencies like a flat tire, a medical co-pay, or unexpected bills.
2. **Builds confidence:** Saving that first chunk of money proves to yourself that you *can* take control of your finances.
3. **Creates momentum:** Once you hit this milestone, you'll feel motivated to aim higher—because now you've seen what's possible.

Micro-Habit: Save $1–$5 a Day

Reaching $500 might feel overwhelming, but here's the secret: You don't have to do it all at once. Small, consistent actions add up faster than you think.

- **Start small:** Commit to saving $1–$5 a day. Whether it's the change from your coffee habit, a few dollars from a side gig, or trimming a small expense, every little bit counts.
- **Make it automatic:** Set up an automatic transfer to a savings account or use a savings app that rounds up your purchases.

If you save just $3 a day, you'll have $500 in less than six months. And if you find ways to save more, you'll get there even faster!

Creative Ways to Find Extra Cash

- **Sell unused items:** That old bike in the garage or the clothes you haven't worn in years could add $50–$100 to your fund.
- **Cut back temporarily:** Skip takeout for a month or pause a subscription service. Redirect those savings to your emergency fund.
- **Pick up a small side hustle:** Babysitting, dog walking, or selling crafts online can help you reach your goal quickly.

Success Stories: Real-Life Wins

Saving $500 might sound small, but for many people, it's been a lifesaver.

- **Maria's story:** "I started putting $5 aside every week, and within a few months, I had $500. When my son needed a last-minute doctor visit, I was able to pay the co-pay without stress. That was a game-changer for me."
- **James's story:** "I sold old tools I wasn't using and saved $300 in a weekend. That gave me the motivation to keep going, and now I have $1,000

saved."

These are regular people who started where you are—and you can do it too.

What Happens When You Have $500 Saved

- **Peace of mind:** You'll sleep better knowing you have a safety net for life's curveballs.
- **A sense of progress:** Hitting that $500 goal proves you can achieve what you set your mind to.
- **A launchpad for bigger goals:** Once you've saved $500, you'll be ready to tackle bigger milestones, like paying off debt or building a larger emergency fund.

Reflection: What Will $500 Mean for You?

Take a moment to think about the last time an unexpected expense stressed you out. How would having $500 set aside have changed that experience?

Now, imagine the next time life throws a surprise your way. Instead of panicking, you'll feel calm and in control because you've got this.

Quick Action Step

1. Set a $500 goal for your emergency fund.
2. Start saving $1–$5 a day. Use a jar, an app, or a separate savings account.
3. Track your progress and celebrate small wins along the way.

You're not just saving money—you're taking the first step toward breaking free from financial stress. This $500 is more than a number; it's a symbol of your commitment to a better future.

Small steps. Big changes. Let's make it happen!

Chapter 5

Learn Something New About Money Every Week

Knowledge is Power—Especially When It Comes to Money

If you've ever felt stuck financially, you're not alone. But here's the truth: Breaking free from the poverty cycle isn't just about earning more or spending less. It's about transforming the way you think about money—and that starts with education.

Financial freedom begins when you empower yourself with knowledge. The more you learn, the better equipped you'll be to make decisions that create lasting wealth. And the best part? You don't need to go back to school or spend hours every day studying. By committing to learning just one new thing about money each week, you can create a ripple effect that changes your life.

Why Financial Education is Crucial

Millions of people grow up without ever learning the basics of money management. Schools don't teach it. Families often avoid talking about it. And yet, money affects every area of our lives.

Financial education is what separates those who stay stuck from those who rise above. When you take the time to learn, you'll discover:

- **How to manage money wisely:** No more guessing where your paycheck went.
- **How to make your money grow:** Through smart saving and investing.
- **How to avoid costly mistakes:** Like high-interest debt or bad investments.

Even one new piece of knowledge can lead to decisions that save you thousands—or even millions—over time.

Micro-Habit: Commit to Weekly Learning

You don't need to become a financial guru overnight. Start small. Dedicate just 30 minutes a week to learning something new about money. Here's how:

- **Read:** Pick one article, blog post, or book chapter each week. Focus on beginner-friendly topics like budgeting, saving, or investing.

- **Listen:** Subscribe to a personal finance podcast and listen while you're commuting, exercising, or cooking.
- **Watch:** Follow a YouTube channel or take a free online course that explains financial concepts in plain language.

In one year, this small habit will add up to 52 new lessons about money—enough to transform your financial outlook.

Resources to Get You Started

Here's a curated list of beginner-friendly resources to jumpstart your financial education:

- **Books:**
    - *The Total Money Makeover* by Dave Ramsey
    - *Rich Dad Poor Dad* by Robert Kiyosaki
    - *Your Money or Your Life* by Vicki Robin
    - *I Will Teach You to Be Rich* by Ramit Sethi
    - *The Millionaire Mindset Blueprint* by Mitchell C. Henderson
    - *The Ultimate Guide to Escaping the Broke Lifestyle* by Mitchell C. Henderson
- **Podcasts:**
    - *Get Rich with Mitch*

- *The Ramsey Show*
- *BiggerPockets Money Podcast*
- *HerMoney with Jean Chatzky*
- *ChooseFI*
- **Websites and Blogs:**
  - NerdWallet.com
  - TheBalance.com
  - MrMoneyMustache.com
  - Smart Passive Income by Pat Flynn
- **YouTube Channels:**
  - Graham Stephan
  - The Financial Diet
  - Andrei Jikh

The Ripple Effect of Consistent Learning

Every time you learn something new about money, you're equipping yourself with tools to make better decisions. That knowledge compounds over time, just like interest on an investment.

For example:

- Learning about compound interest could inspire you to open your first savings or investment account.
- Understanding credit card terms might help you avoid high-interest debt.

- Discovering new budgeting strategies could free up extra money to save or invest.

Each small insight builds on the last, creating momentum that pushes you closer to financial freedom.

Real-Life Example: Sarah's Journey to Financial Freedom

Sarah used to feel completely overwhelmed by money. She lived paycheck to paycheck, avoided looking at her bank statements, and assumed she'd always be broke. Then she decided to learn just one thing about money every week.

In the first month, she learned how to create a simple budget. By the third month, she started paying off her debt using the debt snowball method. A year later, she had $2,000 saved, no credit card debt, and a growing investment account.

Her secret? Small, consistent learning. "It didn't feel like much at first," Sarah says, "but each new thing I learned gave me the confidence to keep going."

Reflection: What Will You Learn This Week?

Ask yourself:

- What's one area of personal finance that confuses me?
- How could learning about it improve my life?
- What resources can I explore this week to get started?

Commit to finding one book, podcast, article, or video that addresses that topic. Take notes, and think about how you can apply what you've learned.

Quick Action Step

1. Choose a topic you want to learn about (e.g., budgeting, debt, or investing).
2. Pick one resource—a book, podcast, article, or video—to dive into this week.
3. Dedicate 30 minutes to learning, and write down one action step based on what you've discovered.

The poverty cycle thrives on ignorance. But the more you educate yourself, the stronger and more confident you become. Remember, this isn't about learning everything all at once—it's about building knowledge over time.

Each week, with every new lesson, you're breaking free. You're stepping into a future where financial freedom isn't just a dream—it's your reality.

Chapter 6
Automate Your Success

Work Smarter, Not Harder

Imagine if your finances could take care of themselves—saving, paying bills, and growing your wealth, all without you lifting a finger. Sounds like a dream, right? The good news is, it's not just possible; it's simple. Automation is one of the most powerful tools in your financial toolkit, and it works because it removes the temptation to overspend, the stress of forgetting, and the excuse of procrastination.

When you automate, you're building a system that works for you in the background. It's like having an assistant who never forgets to put money into savings or pay your bills on time. This micro-habit doesn't just make life easier—it puts you on a steady path to financial success.

The Power of Automation

Here's why automation is such a game-changer:

1. **Saves Time and Energy:** You don't have to think about saving or paying bills every month—it just happens.
2. **Builds Consistency:** Even if it's just $10 a paycheck, those small, regular contributions add up over time.
3. **Eliminates Human Error:** No more missed payments, overdraft fees, or forgetting to save.
4. **Reduces Temptation:** When money is transferred to savings automatically, you're less likely to spend it.

Automation isn't about being lazy—it's about being smart. It's about using technology to create financial habits that stick.

Micro-Habit: Automate Your Savings

If saving money feels like a struggle, automation can make it effortless. Start with a small, achievable amount—just $10 per paycheck is enough to get the ball rolling.

Here's how to set it up:

1. **Choose a Savings Goal:** Is it your $500 emergency fund? A new laptop? A future vacation?

Having a goal makes the habit more motivating.
2. **Set Up Automatic Transfers:** Log into your bank's website or app and schedule an automatic transfer to your savings account every time you get paid.
3. **Start Small:** Even if it's just $10, the key is to start. You can always increase the amount later.

Micro-Habit: Automate Your Bills

Late fees and missed payments are a drain on your finances and your peace of mind. Automation ensures your bills are paid on time, every time.

Here's how to do it:

1. **List Your Bills:** Write down all recurring bills—rent, utilities, insurance, subscriptions, etc.
2. **Set Up Auto-Pay:** Most companies offer auto-pay options through their websites. You can also use your bank's bill-pay feature to manage everything in one place.
3. **Monitor Your Account:** Check your account regularly to ensure there's enough money to cover automated payments.

Tools to Make Automation Easy

Technology has made financial automation easier than ever. Here are some tools to help you get started:

- **Bank Apps:** Most banks allow you to schedule automatic transfers and payments directly through their app or website.
- **Savings Apps:** Apps like Acorns, Digit, and Qapital can round up your purchases and save the spare change automatically.
- **Budgeting Apps:** Tools like Mint and YNAB (You Need a Budget) help you track and manage your automated systems.
- **Direct Deposit Splits:** Many employers allow you to split your paycheck into multiple accounts. Set up a portion to go directly into savings.

Staying Consistent

Automation is a "set it and forget it" strategy, but it still requires some oversight to ensure it's working as intended. Make it a habit to check in on your finances once a month:

- Review your bank statements to confirm that transfers and payments are happening as scheduled.

- Adjust your savings amount as your income increases or your goals change.
- Celebrate your progress—seeing your savings grow or your bills being handled smoothly is incredibly motivating.

Real-Life Example: Alex's Savings Breakthrough

Alex always struggled to save. Every time she tried, something came up—a last-minute bill, an impulse buy, or a social outing she didn't want to miss. Then she discovered automation.

She set up her bank to transfer $20 from every paycheck into a separate savings account. At first, it didn't feel like much, but she stuck with it. Six months later, Alex checked her account and was shocked to see $240 saved without even thinking about it.

"It felt like magic," Alex said. "I wasn't stressed about saving because it was automatic. Now, I'm upping it to $50 per paycheck!"

Reflection: What Can You Automate Today?

Ask yourself:

- What's one small savings goal I can automate this week?

- Which bills could I put on auto-pay to simplify my finances?
- How can I use automation to make financial progress effortless?

Quick Action Step

1. Log into your bank account and set up an automatic transfer for your chosen savings amount.
2. Choose one recurring bill and set it to auto-pay through your bank or the biller's website.
3. Download a savings or budgeting app to help you track and adjust your automated habits.

Your Financial Success on Autopilot

Automation is like planting seeds for your future. It's a simple, powerful way to ensure you're making progress even when life gets busy. With every automated transfer, every bill paid on time, you're proving to yourself that financial freedom isn't just a dream—it's a system you can build and trust.

Remember, the goal isn't perfection—it's progress. Automate your success today, and let your money work for you while you focus on living your life.

Chapter 7
Invest in Yourself

Your Greatest Asset is You

When people think about investments, they often picture stocks, real estate, or retirement accounts. But the most valuable investment you can make isn't found on Wall Street—it's you. Building your skills, expanding your knowledge, and developing yourself personally and professionally are the most powerful ways to increase your earning potential and secure your financial future.

Unlike traditional investments, which can fluctuate with the market, the return on investing in yourself is consistent and exponential. A new skill could lead to a higher-paying job. A certification could open doors to a promotion. Even reading a single book could inspire an idea that changes the trajectory of your life.

When you prioritize your growth, you're not just breaking the poverty cycle—you're building a life that's rich in opportunity, confidence, and purpose.

The Compounding Effect of Knowledge

Think of knowledge like compound interest. Each small piece of learning builds on the last, multiplying over time into a wealth of expertise. The key is consistency. You don't need to dedicate hours every day to see results; even 15 minutes of focused effort can create life-changing progress.

Here's why investing in yourself matters:

- **Boosts Earning Potential:** The more skills you have, the more value you bring to employers, clients, or your own business.
- **Increases Job Security:** In a competitive job market, having additional skills or certifications can set you apart.
- **Fuels Confidence:** Learning and growing empower you to tackle challenges and seize new opportunities.
- **Builds Independence:** By improving your knowledge, you rely less on others and more on your own capabilities.

Micro-Habit: Dedicate 15 Minutes a Day to Learning

You don't need to overhaul your life to start investing in yourself. Begin with just 15 minutes a day—small, manageable chunks of time that add up to meaningful progress.

Here's how to make it happen:

1. **Pick a Focus:** What skill or topic would have the biggest impact on your life right now? Maybe it's budgeting, coding, marketing, or communication.
2. **Choose Your Method:** Read a book, listen to a podcast, watch a YouTube tutorial, or take an online course.
3. **Make it Routine:** Set a timer for 15 minutes and commit to it daily. Consistency is more important than intensity.

Free or Low-Cost Resources for Growth

You don't need to spend a fortune to invest in yourself. There are countless free or affordable resources that can help you level up:

- **Free Online Courses:** Platforms like Coursera, edX, and Khan Academy offer high-quality courses from top universities.
- **YouTube Tutorials:** Learn everything from Excel to graphic design to cooking for free.
- **Public Libraries:** Many libraries provide access to free books, e-books, and even online learning resources like LinkedIn Learning.

- **Community Programs:** Check local organizations or community colleges for free or low-cost workshops and classes.
- **Podcasts and Blogs:** Find experts in your area of interest and learn from their experiences and insights.

Examples of Skill-Building Opportunities

Here are a few ways you can start investing in yourself today:

- **Learn a Marketable Skill:** Coding, graphic design, social media management, or data analysis can open doors to better-paying opportunities.
- **Earn a Certification:** Many fields, like IT, healthcare, or project management, offer certifications that can lead to higher salaries.
- **Improve Communication Skills:** Mastering public speaking or writing can boost your career prospects and personal relationships.
- **Start a Side Hustle:** Experimenting with freelance work or entrepreneurship teaches valuable lessons while increasing your income.
- **Hone Your Financial Literacy:** Understanding personal finance can help you make smarter money decisions and achieve your goals faster.

Real-Life Example: Maya's Career Leap

Maya worked long hours at a minimum-wage job, dreaming of a better life but unsure how to get there. One day, she decided to dedicate just 15 minutes a day to learning. She started with free YouTube tutorials on graphic design, a skill she'd always admired but never pursued.

Over time, her 15 minutes grew into an hour, and her confidence grew too. Within six months, she built a small portfolio and started taking on freelance projects. A year later, Maya landed a full-time job as a graphic designer, doubling her income and finally escaping the paycheck-to-paycheck cycle.

"It all started with those 15 minutes," Maya said. "I didn't realize how much I could change my life by just starting small."

Reflection: What Will You Learn Next?

Ask yourself:

- What skill could make the biggest difference in my life right now?
- How can I dedicate 15 minutes a day to learning and growth?
- What free or low-cost resources are available to me today?

Quick Action Step

1. Write down one skill or area you'd like to improve.
2. Find a free or affordable resource to help you get started (like a podcast, book, or online course).
3. Commit to spending 15 minutes today learning something new.

Your Growth is the Key to Your Freedom

Investing in yourself is the most empowering step you can take to break the poverty cycle. Every skill you build, every new concept you learn, and every minute you dedicate to growth is a step closer to the life you want.

Remember, it's not about perfection or massive leaps—it's about small, consistent actions that lead to big, transformative results. You are your greatest asset. Start investing today, and watch your life change for the better.

Chapter 8
Practice Gratitude and Financial Mindset Shifts

Abundance Over Scarcity

When you're stuck in the cycle of financial struggle, it's easy to view the world through the lens of scarcity—there's never enough money, opportunities, or time. But this mindset doesn't just reflect your circumstances; it reinforces them. Constantly focusing on lack creates stress, fear, and decision paralysis. To break free, you need to shift your perspective from scarcity to abundance.

Abundance doesn't mean pretending everything is perfect or ignoring your challenges. It's about recognizing the resources, opportunities, and blessings you already have. When you approach life with gratitude and a focus on abundance, you're more likely to make confident, positive decisions that lead to growth and financial stability.

Why Gratitude Changes Everything

Gratitude isn't just a feel-good emotion—it's a powerful tool for rewiring your brain. Research shows that practicing gratitude can reduce stress, improve mental health, and even enhance your financial decision-making. When you focus on what you're grateful for, you break the cycle of negative thinking and open your mind to possibilities and solutions.

Here's how gratitude can transform your financial mindset:

- **Shifts Your Focus:** Instead of dwelling on what you don't have, you start appreciating what you do have.
- **Encourages Better Choices:** Gratitude fosters patience and long-term thinking, which are essential for saving and investing.
- **Builds Resilience:** Recognizing your blessings helps you weather financial setbacks with a positive outlook.
- **Boosts Confidence:** When you're grateful for your progress, no matter how small, you feel empowered to keep going.

Micro-Habit: Three Things You're Grateful For

You don't need hours of meditation or a fancy journal to practice gratitude. Start with a simple habit: every day, write down three things you're grateful for.

These can be small, like:

- "I have food on the table today."
- "I learned something new from a podcast."
- "I was able to pay a bill on time."

Or they can be bigger milestones:

- "I saved $100 toward my emergency fund."
- "I got a freelance gig that helps with extra income."
- "I spent meaningful time with my family."

The key is consistency. This daily habit helps retrain your brain to focus on the positive, no matter how challenging your financial situation might seem.

From Scarcity to Empowerment

When you focus on scarcity, you're more likely to make fear-based decisions: splurging to feel a momentary sense of relief, avoiding budgeting because it seems overwhelming, or giving up on your goals because they feel too far away. Gratitude flips the script.

Instead of saying:

- "I'll never get ahead," you say, "I've made progress, and I can make more."
- "There's no way to save money," you say, "I'm grateful I saved $10 this week."
- "I'm so far behind," you say, "I'm thankful I've taken the first step."

How Gratitude Leads to Better Financial Decisions

Practicing gratitude isn't just about feeling good—it has practical benefits for your financial journey:

- **Improved Impulse Control:** When you focus on what you already have, you're less likely to chase fleeting happiness through unnecessary purchases.
- **Clarity in Goals:** Gratitude helps you prioritize what truly matters, so your spending aligns with your values.
- **Increased Motivation:** Celebrating small wins fuels your drive to keep moving forward.
- **Stronger Relationships:** Gratitude fosters kindness and generosity, which can lead to support and opportunities in your financial journey.

A Real-Life Example: Carla's Gratitude Practice

Carla was drowning in debt and felt overwhelmed by her financial struggles. Every day, she focused on what she couldn't afford and how far behind she was, which only made her feel more stuck.

One day, a friend suggested she start a gratitude journal. Skeptical but desperate for change, Carla gave it a try. At first, it felt silly to write, "I'm grateful for the roof over my head" when her financial problems loomed so large. But over time, she began to notice a shift.

She stopped fixating on her lack and started appreciating her progress. She celebrated every small win: a $50 debt payment, a $20 savings deposit, a new budgeting skill. With her new mindset, Carla felt motivated to tackle her finances head-on. Within two years, she paid off her credit card debt, built a $1,000 emergency fund, and even started investing.

Reflection: Your Gratitude Journey

Ask yourself:

- What three things am I grateful for right now, no matter how small?
- How can gratitude shift my focus from lack to abundance?
- How can I celebrate the progress I've already made on my financial journey?

Quick Action Step

1. Start a gratitude practice today. Write down three things you're grateful for—on paper, in your phone, or even mentally.
2. Repeat this habit daily, building a positive mindset that fuels your financial success.

Your Future, Fueled by Gratitude

Gratitude isn't about ignoring the hard work ahead—it's about empowering yourself to move forward with hope, strength, and confidence. By focusing on what you have instead of what you lack, you're setting the foundation for a mindset that attracts growth and abundance.

Your journey to financial freedom isn't just about numbers—it's about the mindset you bring to the table. Start practicing gratitude today, and watch how this small habit transforms not only your finances but your entire outlook on life.

Chapter 9
The 10% Rule for Giving Back

Generosity: A Key to Financial Freedom

It might seem counterintuitive to talk about giving when you're working to break free from financial struggles. After all, how can you afford to give when every dollar feels essential? The truth is, generosity isn't just an act of kindness—it's a powerful way to shift your mindset and reclaim control over your money.

When you give, no matter how small the amount, you send a message to yourself: *I have enough.* This simple act helps break the chains of scarcity thinking and cultivates a mindset of abundance. Giving is not about the size of the gift; it's about the heart behind it.

The Power of the 10% Rule

The "10% Rule" is a principle many financially free individuals live by: setting aside a portion of their income, often 10%, to give back. But if 10% feels overwhelming right now, start smaller—maybe $1 a month, $5 a paycheck, or even a few coins in a jar. The point is to create a habit of generosity that grows with you.

Here's why this rule works:

- **It Builds Discipline:** Allocating even a tiny percentage of your income for giving helps you stay intentional with your finances.
- **It Creates Gratitude:** When you give, you're reminded of what you have to be thankful for.
- **It Inspires Growth:** Generosity cultivates a mindset of abundance, which helps you see opportunities instead of limitations.

Micro-Habit: Start Small, Start Today

Don't wait until you're debt-free or financially stable to start giving. Even $1 a month can make a difference. Here's how to begin:

1. Choose a cause you care about—something that aligns with your values.
2. Commit to a specific amount, no matter how small.
3. Set up an automatic donation or make it part of your budget.

The act of giving isn't just about helping others; it's about transforming your relationship with money.

The Ripple Effect of Generosity

Generosity has a way of creating ripples that extend far beyond the initial gift. When you give, you inspire others to do the same. You contribute to a cycle of positivity and abundance that can uplift entire communities.

Consider this:

- A small donation to a food bank might feed a family for a day, easing their burden and giving them hope.
- Contributing to an education fund might help a child discover new possibilities.
- Supporting a local business or artist might give them the boost they need to succeed.

These ripples not only impact others but also reinforce your belief in your ability to make a difference—no matter where you are in your financial journey.

The Science of Giving: Why It Feels Good

Studies show that acts of generosity release dopamine, the "feel-good" chemical in your brain. Giving doesn't just benefit the recipient—it improves your mental health, reduces stress, and boosts happiness. It's a reminder that financial freedom isn't just about accumulating wealth; it's about living a life of purpose and joy.

Real-Life Example: James' Giving Journey

James was deep in debt and living paycheck to paycheck when a friend challenged him to start giving back. Skeptical but curious, he decided to donate $5 a month to a local animal shelter.

At first, the amount felt insignificant, but over time, James noticed something changing. He felt a sense of pride and purpose knowing he was making a difference, no matter how small. This mindset shift gave him the motivation to tackle his finances with renewed energy. Within a year, James increased his giving to $20 a month and had also paid off two credit cards.

"I thought I needed to wait until I was financially stable to give," James said, "but giving helped me get there faster."

Reflection: Your Generosity Goals

Ask yourself:
- What cause or community am I passionate about supporting?

- How can I incorporate giving into my current financial plan, even if it's just $1 a month?
- How might generosity change the way I view money and abundance?

Quick Action Step

1. Choose a cause you care about.
2. Commit to giving a small amount—$1, $5, or whatever you can afford.
3. Reflect on how giving makes you feel and the impact it creates.

Abundance Through Giving

When you give, you remind yourself that you are not defined by your bank balance. Generosity isn't about waiting until you "have enough"—it's about recognizing that *you already do.* It's a declaration that your life is about more than survival; it's about thriving and making a difference.

The habit of giving doesn't just transform your finances—it transforms your heart. By embracing generosity, you unlock a life of purpose, abundance, and joy. Start today, and let your giving create ripples that change the world.

Chapter 10
Dream Big, Plan Small

The Balance Between Vision and Action

Every great achievement starts with a dream. Whether it's owning your own home, starting a business, paying for your child's education, or retiring comfortably, dreams give us direction and purpose. But dreams alone won't change your life—it's the small, consistent actions you take every day that turn those dreams into reality.

This chapter is about bridging the gap between where you are and where you want to be. It's about taking that big, bold dream and breaking it into manageable steps. By dreaming big and planning small, you set yourself up for success without feeling overwhelmed.

Why Goals Matter

Setting financial goals isn't just about the numbers—it's about creating a vision for your future. Goals give you a reason to stay disciplined, a purpose for your sacrifices, and motivation to keep going when the road gets tough.

Think about it:

- Without a goal, saving money feels like a chore.
- With a goal, every dollar saved feels like progress toward something meaningful.

Your goals can be as small as paying off one bill or as big as traveling the world debt-free. What matters is that they're clear, actionable, and aligned with your values.

Micro-Habit: Write Down One Financial Dream

Let's start with a simple exercise: write down one financial dream you have. Maybe it's something you've been thinking about for years but haven't had the courage to act on.

Once you've identified your dream, ask yourself:

1. **Why does this matter to me?** Connecting your goal to your values and emotions will keep you motivated.
2. **What's the first baby step I can take today?** Breaking your dream into small, actionable steps makes it feel achievable.

For example:

- Dream: Save $10,000 for a down payment on a home.

- Baby Step: Open a high-yield savings account and transfer $50 to it this week.

The Power of Visualization

Visualization is a powerful tool for achieving your goals. When you clearly picture yourself reaching your dream, it becomes more tangible and attainable.

Take a few minutes to close your eyes and imagine what life will look like when you achieve your goal. Picture the house you'll buy, the freedom of being debt-free, or the joy of treating your family to a vacation. The more vivid your vision, the more motivated you'll be to take action.

Planning Small: Breaking Down Big Goals

Here's how to turn your financial dream into a series of baby steps:

1. **Define Your Goal:** Be specific. Instead of "save more money," try "save $5,000 for an emergency fund in two years."
2. **Set a Timeline:** Break your goal into smaller milestones. For example, saving $5,000 in two years means saving about $210 a month.
3. **Take the First Step:** Focus on what you can do today, no matter how small. Starting builds momentum.

Celebrating Small Wins

One of the keys to staying motivated is celebrating your progress along the way. Every time you hit a milestone, take a moment to acknowledge your achievement. Whether it's saving your first $500, paying off a small debt, or sticking to your budget for a month, these wins matter.

Celebrations don't have to cost money—write yourself a note of encouragement, share your success with a friend, or treat yourself to a quiet moment of reflection. Recognizing your progress reminds you that you're capable of achieving even more.

Real-Life Example: Maria's Dream of Debt Freedom

Maria dreamed of being debt-free but felt overwhelmed by the $20,000 she owed. Instead of focusing on the total, she started with a small goal: paying off one credit card with a $500 balance.

She committed to cutting back on dining out and used that money to make extra payments. Within three months, the $500 card was gone. Motivated by her success, Maria tackled the next card, and the next.

Four years later, Maria became completely debt-free. "It all started with one small step," she said. "That first win gave me the confidence to keep going."

Reflection: What's Your Dream?

Take a moment to reflect on your own financial dreams:

- What is one financial goal you've always wanted to achieve?
- Why is this dream important to you?
- What's one small step you can take today to move closer to it?

Quick Action Step

1. Write down your financial dream.
2. Break it into baby steps with clear milestones.
3. Take the first step today, no matter how small.

Dream Big, Plan Small, Achieve Greatness

Your dreams are worth pursuing. They're worth the effort, discipline, and sacrifices required to achieve them. But remember, the path to greatness isn't about taking giant leaps—it's about consistent, small steps that add up over time.

When you dream big and plan small, you create a roadmap to the life you've always wanted. Stay focused, stay inspired, and keep moving forward. Your financial freedom is closer than you think.

Chapter 11
The Power of Community

You're Not Alone

The journey to financial freedom can feel isolating at times. When you're saying no to outings, cutting back on luxuries, or focusing on paying off debt while others around you seem to spend freely, it's easy to feel like the odd one out. But here's the truth: You don't have to do this alone.

One of the most powerful tools on your journey to breaking the poverty cycle is community. Surrounding yourself with like-minded individuals who share your goals can provide encouragement, accountability, and wisdom to keep you moving forward.

Why Community Matters

No one climbs a mountain alone. Every great success story involves a network of people—mentors, friends, family, or peers—who provide guidance, support, and accountability. Financial freedom is no different.

Here's what a strong community can do for you:

1. **Encouragement:** When setbacks happen (and they will), having people who understand your journey can keep you motivated.
2. **Accountability:** Sharing your goals with someone means you're more likely to follow through.
3. **Shared Wisdom:** Learning from others' experiences can save you time and effort.

Finding Your Tribe

Your community doesn't have to be large or formal. It could be as simple as a friend who shares your financial goals or a group of coworkers interested in budgeting tips. What matters is that you're connecting with people who encourage and inspire you to keep going.

Here are a few places to find like-minded individuals:

- **Online Forums and Social Media Groups:** Platforms like Reddit (e.g., r/personalfinance) or Facebook groups focused on budgeting or debt repayment.
- **Local Meetups:** Check for workshops or community groups focused on financial literacy.
- **Faith-Based or Community Organizations:** Many churches and nonprofits host financial

peace or budgeting classes.
- **Accountability Partnerships:** Find one person you trust—whether a friend, spouse, or mentor—and commit to checking in regularly.

Micro-Habit: Share One Goal for Accountability

A small but powerful habit is to share one of your financial goals with someone you trust. This could be as simple as saying, "I want to save $500 for an emergency fund by the end of the year."

Why does this matter? Sharing your goals makes them real. It shifts them from a private thought to a shared commitment, and when you know someone else is rooting for you, it becomes easier to stay on track.

Success Story: James and Lisa's Accountability Partnership

James and Lisa, coworkers and friends, both wanted to break free from the paycheck-to-paycheck cycle. One day, during a lunch break, they decided to hold each other accountable for their financial goals.

Each month, they met to review their budgets, celebrate wins, and share lessons learned. James found that having someone cheer him on helped him stay disciplined, while Lisa appreciated James's practical advice.

In two years, both James and Lisa paid off their credit card debt and started investing. They credit their success to the power of their accountability partnership.

Resources: Communities to Join

Here are some starting points to find your financial freedom community:

- **Books and Authors:** Follow authors or financial experts who offer group challenges or online communities.
- **Podcasts:** Many finance podcasts have dedicated listener groups.
- **Financial Peace University (Dave Ramsey):** A popular program that offers group-based classes.
- **Local Libraries or Colleges:** Many host free financial literacy workshops.

Reflection: Who's in Your Corner?

Take a moment to think about the people in your life. Who can you turn to for encouragement or advice on your financial journey? If no one comes to mind, that's okay—this is an opportunity to expand your network.

Ask yourself:

- Who shares similar goals or values?

- Who do I trust to provide honest and constructive feedback?
- Where can I find a community of like-minded individuals?

Quick Action Step

1. Identify one financial goal you're currently working on.
2. Share that goal with someone you trust and ask them to check in with you in a week or month.
3. Find one online or local financial community to join and connect with others.

Building a Legacy of Support

Community isn't just about receiving help—it's also about giving back. As you make progress on your journey, you'll find opportunities to inspire and support others. Whether it's sharing a budgeting tip with a friend, mentoring someone starting out, or simply celebrating another's progress, you'll experience the joy of paying it forward.

Together, we rise. When you surround yourself with a supportive community, the impossible becomes achievable, and the journey feels a little lighter. Financial freedom isn't just about personal success—it's about creating a ripple effect that lifts others up, too.

Your Financial Freedom Squad Awaits

Start building your tribe today. Share your dreams, find encouragement, and become the inspiration someone else needs. Together, we can break the cycle and create a future full of abundance, one step at a time.

Chapter 12
Consistency Over Perfection

The Myth of Perfection

When we think about success, it's easy to fall into the trap of believing we need to do everything perfectly. We imagine flawless budgets, savings growing effortlessly, and never making a financial mistake again. But the truth? Financial freedom isn't about perfection—it's about showing up consistently, even when it's hard.

Perfection sets an impossible standard that can lead to frustration and quitting. Consistency, however, builds momentum. It's about taking one step every day, no matter how small, and trusting that those steps will add up over time.

Why Consistency Wins Every Time

Think about it: Does it matter if you save $1 every day instead of $100 all at once? Absolutely not. What matters is building the habit of saving. Consistency works like compound interest—it takes small actions and multiplies their impact over time.

Here's why consistency is your greatest ally:

1. **It Builds Habits:** Repeating small actions daily rewires your brain, making good financial habits automatic.
2. **It Reduces Overwhelm:** Small steps feel manageable, while trying to do everything at once can feel paralyzing.
3. **It Creates Results:** The secret to success isn't massive leaps—it's steady, daily progress.

Micro-Habit: One Action, Every Day

Pick one financial habit you want to work on and commit to doing it daily. Maybe it's saving $1, tracking expenses, or reading a financial article. It doesn't have to be big—what matters is the daily practice.

By focusing on one habit, you build confidence and momentum. Over time, that one habit becomes part of who you are, making it easier to stack more good habits on top.

Celebrate Your Wins

Too often, we focus on what we haven't done yet instead of celebrating how far we've come. But acknowledging your progress is crucial—it keeps you motivated and reminds you of your capacity to grow and improve.

Take a moment to reflect on your journey so far:

- Did you open a savings account?
- Cut out one unnecessary expense?
- Start tracking your spending?

Each step is worth celebrating because it's proof that you're moving forward.

Success Story: Maria's Journey to Consistency

Maria felt overwhelmed by her financial situation. She had debt, no savings, and no idea where to start. At first, she tried to overhaul her entire life in one week, but it didn't last—she burned out quickly.

Then she decided to focus on one habit: saving $1 every day. It felt so small that it seemed almost silly, but Maria stayed consistent. Over time, $1 turned into $5, and $5 turned into $20. Within six months, she had saved $500—her first emergency fund.

Maria's journey wasn't perfect. There were days she missed saving, and she occasionally splurged on things she didn't need. But she learned that the key wasn't perfection—it was consistency.

Reflection: Progress Over Perfection

Take a moment to reflect on what consistency could look like for you. Ask yourself:

- What is one small, daily habit I can commit to right now?
- How can I remind myself to stay consistent?
- What progress have I already made that I can celebrate today?

Remember, it's not about never making mistakes. It's about showing up, learning, and continuing to move forward.

Your Financial Journey Is Yours

It's tempting to compare yourself to others, especially in today's world of curated social media highlights. But your journey is uniquely yours. Focus on your progress, not someone else's timeline.

Quick Action Step

1. Choose one financial habit to practice daily.
2. Write it down where you'll see it every day.

3. Celebrate small wins—track your progress and reward yourself for sticking with it.

Consistency Creates Transformation

Imagine where you'll be a year from now if you commit to consistent, daily action. Even if you miss a day here or there, your efforts will compound over time.

Financial freedom isn't about having a perfect record. It's about persistence, resilience, and believing in your ability to create a better future.

Celebrate How Far You've Come

As you finish this chapter, take a moment to recognize how far you've come—not just in this book, but in your journey toward breaking the poverty cycle.

The steps you've taken may feel small, but they're part of something much bigger: a transformation in how you think about money, your habits, and your future.

You've proven to yourself that you can do this. And the best part? This is just the beginning.

Keep showing up, one day at a time. Consistency over perfection will carry you further than you ever imagined. Your journey to financial freedom is well underway, and the best is yet to come.

Conclusion
Freedom is Within Reach

The Journey of a Thousand Miles

You've taken a big step just by reading this book. You've equipped yourself with the tools, strategies, and mindset to break free from the cycle of poverty. But let's be clear: real change doesn't come from reading—it comes from doing.

The good news? The journey to financial freedom doesn't require giant leaps. It's built on small, consistent actions—micro-habits—that compound over time. Each step you take, no matter how small, brings you closer to your goals.

The Power of Progress

As we've seen throughout this book, financial freedom isn't about perfection. It's about showing up, trying, and taking the next step forward, even when it feels hard.

- Did you save your first dollar? That's progress.

- Did you track your spending for a week? That's progress.
- Did you redirect even one unnecessary expense toward savings or debt repayment? That's progress.

Celebrate those victories. They're proof that you're moving in the right direction.

One Habit at a Time

When you think about everything we've covered—saving, budgeting, investing, cutting expenses, learning, and giving—it might feel overwhelming. But here's the secret: you don't need to do it all at once.

Start with one habit. Just one. Maybe it's saving $1 a day, tracking your expenses, or committing to learning something new about money each week. Whatever it is, make it your focus. Build consistency. Once that habit feels natural, add another.

This journey isn't a sprint—it's a marathon. And the beauty of small steps is that they're sustainable.

Freedom is a Choice

Financial freedom isn't reserved for the lucky or the privileged. It's available to anyone willing to take consistent, intentional action. That includes you.

Yes, there will be challenges along the way. Yes, there will be setbacks. But those moments don't define your journey. What matters is how you respond—how you get back up, recommit, and keep moving forward.

You've already proven that you're capable of change. You've proven it by picking up this book, by engaging with these ideas, and by envisioning a better future for yourself.

Your Next Step Starts Today

So, what will you do next?

- Will you start tracking your expenses?
- Will you open a savings account?
- Will you commit to learning something new about money this week?

Whatever it is, start today. Not tomorrow. Not next week. Today. Because every day you delay is a day you could have been one step closer to freedom.

Your Financial Freedom Story

Imagine yourself a year from now. Picture the progress you'll have made if you commit to even one habit. See yourself with less stress, more security, and greater confidence in your financial future.

That vision can be your reality. But it starts with one small step—and it starts now.

Final Call to Action

Choose one habit from this book. Write it down. Commit to it.

Then take the first step. Put this book down and take action.

Your freedom is within reach. It's waiting for you to claim it, one small, consistent step at a time.

You've got this. The journey begins now.

Bonus Material 1
Habit Tracker Templates

Use these templates to stay consistent and accountable on your financial freedom journey. Track your progress daily, weekly, and monthly to celebrate wins and identify areas for improvement.

Daily Habit Tracker

Date	Habit	Completed? (✔/✘)	Notes
	Save $1		
	Track expenses		
	Read/learn something new		

Weekly Habit Tracker

Week of:	Habit	Completed Days	Notes
Save $1 a day			
Cook one meal at home			
Review spending habits			

Monthly Habit Tracker

Month:	Habit	Completed Weeks	Notes
Add to emergency fund			
Learn one new financial concept			
Reflect on gratitude (weekly)			

Bonus Material 2
Reflection Questions

Use these prompts to dig deeper into your financial habits, goals, and mindset. Write your answers in a journal or discuss them with someone you trust to gain even more clarity.

Your Starting Point
1. What's one financial habit you're excited to start? Why?
2. What's the biggest challenge you face when it comes to money?
3. How does living paycheck-to-paycheck affect your emotional well-being?

Breaking the Poverty Cycle
1. What does financial freedom look like to you?
2. How will breaking the poverty cycle change your life and the legacy you leave for future generations?

3. What's one financial mistake you've made, and what did you learn from it?

Motivation and Progress
1. Who inspires you to work toward financial freedom? Why?
2. What's one financial milestone you've achieved that you're proud of?
3. What's one thing you can do this week to move closer to your financial goals?

www.ingramcontent.com/pod-product-compliance
Lightning Source LLC
Chambersburg PA
CBHW070356230526
45471CB00006B/2595